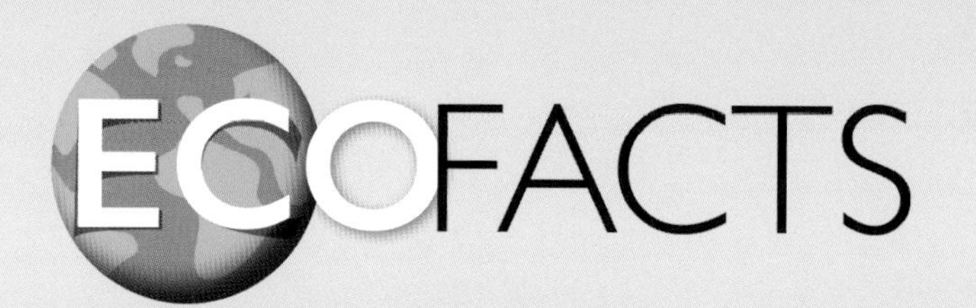

ENERGY

ECO FACTS

IZZI HOWELL

Author: Izzi Howell

Editorial director: Kathy Middleton

Editors: Izzi Howell, Ellen Rodger

Proofreader: Melissa Boyce

Designer: Clare Nicholas

Cover designer: Steve Mead

Prepress technician: Tammy McGarr

Print coordinator: Katherine Berti

Photo credits:
Getty: rvimages 7, Jim West 15, tonda 16, BerndBrueggemann 23; Shutterstock: Oil and Gas Photographer 8, Dmitry Birin 11, chinasong 12, Francois BOIZOT 17, Mykola Gomeniuk 18, Hari Mahidhar 20, dvoevnore 27, Sebastian Noethlichs 29.

All design elements from Shutterstock.

Library and Archives Canada Cataloguing in Publication

Title: Energy eco facts / Izzi Howell.
Names: Howell, Izzi, author.
Description: Series statement: Eco facts | Includes index.
Identifiers: Canadiana (print) 20190087935 |
Canadiana (ebook) 20190087943
ISBN 9780778763468 (hardcover)
ISBN 9780778763628 (softcover)
ISBN 9781427123442 (HTML)
Subjects: LCSH: Power resources—Environmental aspects—Juvenile literature. | LCSH: Energy consumption—Environmental aspects—Juvenile literature. | LCSH: Nature—Effect of human beings on—Juvenile literature.
Classification: LCC TJ163.23 .H69 2019 | DDC j333.79—dc23

Library of Congress Cataloging-in-Publication Data

Names: Howell, Izzi, author.
Title: Energy eco facts / Izzi Howell.
Description: New York : Crabtree Publishing Company, 2019. |
Series: Eco facts | Includes index. |
Audience: Age 10-14+ | Audience: Grade 7 to 8. |
Identifiers: LCCN 2019014214 (print) | LCCN 2019021711 (ebook) |
ISBN 9781427123442 (Electronic) |
ISBN 9780778763468 (hardcover) |
ISBN 9780778763628 (pbk.)
Subjects: LCSH: Power resources--Juvenile literature. |
Power resources--Environmental aspects--Juvenile literature.
Classification: LCC TJ163.23 (ebook) | LCC TJ163.23 .H68 2019 (print) |
DDC 333.79--dc23
LC record available at https://lccn.loc.gov/2019014214

Crabtree Publishing Company

www.crabtreebooks.com 1–800–387–7650

Published by Crabtree Publishing Company in 2020

Printed in the U.S.A./072019/CG20190501

Published in Canada
Crabtree Publishing
616 Welland Ave.
St. Catharines, Ontario
L2M 5V6

Published in the United States
Crabtree Publishing
PMB 59051
350 Fifth Avenue, 59th Floor
New York, New York 10118

Contents

What is energy?

Energy makes things work. It can come from different sources, such as heat, light, and movement. We use energy to power buildings, vehicles, and machines.

Electricity

Electricity is a form of energy. We measure electricity in units such as kilowatt hours (kWh). 1 kWh is the equivalent of using a shower for six minutes or three hours of watching TV. The electricity that we use is generated from different energy resources, such as fossil fuels that are burned in power plants or Sun or wind power.

Renewable or nonrenewable

Energy resources can be **renewable** or **nonrenewable**. Renewable resources can be replaced and will never run out. They include the Sun, wind, water, **geothermal** heat (heat from inside Earth) and **biomass** (natural materials). We have a fixed amount of nonrenewable resources, such as coal, oil, natural gas, and nuclear fuels (see pages 6–9). Supplies of nonrenewable resources are running low and will eventually run out if we don't manage them **sustainably**.

The environment

Generating electricity has a huge impact on the environment. Every stage of the process, from **extracting** and processing energy resources to generating electricity and dealing with waste, damages Earth. Burning **fossil fuels** releases **greenhouse gases** such as carbon dioxide (CO_2). Greenhouse gases gather in the **atmosphere** and trap heat energy from the Sun. This is contributing to global warming. Generating electricity also creates pollution (see page 7).

greenhouse gases

This graph presents the amount that each energy resource contributes to the **greenhouse effect**. It shows how much CO_2 is produced for every kWh generated by different energy resources.

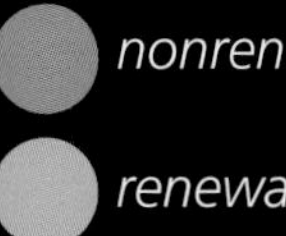

nonrenewable energy

renewable energy

CO_2 in grams

0
200
400
600
800

coal
natural gas
biomass
solar panel
geothermal
concentrated solar power
hydroelectric
offshore wind
nuclear

Fossil fuels

Fossil fuels include natural gas, oil, and coal. They are a popular source of energy, used as a fuel for machines and to generate electricity in power stations. However, there are many drawbacks to using fossil fuels for energy.

Formation

Fossil fuels formed in the ground over millions of years. They are called fossil fuels because they are made up of the remains of ancient plants and animals. Fossil fuels are nonrenewable. When the supply runs out, there will be no more fossil fuels.

This is how oil and gas are formed over millions of years. Coal is also formed underground from the remains of dead plants.

Dead plants and animals fall to the bottom of the ocean.

Mud builds up above the remains.

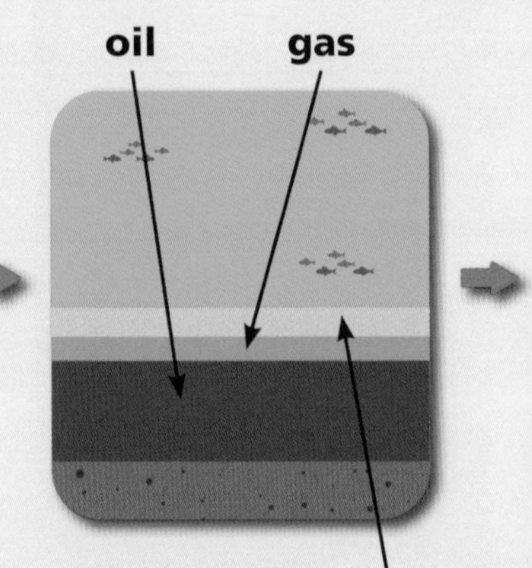

As more mud and rock build up on top of the remains, heat and pressure turn the remains into oil and gas.

History

Fossil fuels have been used since ancient times. Coal was used in China as early as 1000–901 B.C.E. During the Industrial Revolution in the 1700s, huge quantities of fossil fuels began to be used to power the new machines and factories. Since then, the invention of electricity and cars has greatly increased the environmental impact of fossil fuels.

Reasons for use

Fossil fuels are used as a source of energy for several reasons. It is simple to use them to generate electricity (see below) or as a fuel for vehicles, and they produce a huge amount of power. In some areas of the world, they are cheap to find and extract. Most countries already have operational fossil fuel power plants, so they do not need to invest in new technology to supply homes and businesses with power.

An coal power plant in India sends clouds of smoke into the air. Coal supplied 80 percent of India's power in 2016–2017, but it is increasingly being replaced by lower cost wind and solar power.

Fossil fuel plants

The turbine generates electricity.

The turbine powers a generator.

Steam moves a **turbine**.

The boiling water produces steam.

This creates heat, which is used to boil water.

Fossil fuels are burned in power plants.

Gases

When fossil fuels are burned, they release carbon dioxide, which contributes to the greenhouse effect (see page 5). They also give out sulfur dioxide, which creates acid rain that damages plants and buildings. Particulate matter (tiny solid particles of different materials) is also found in fossil fuel smoke. This creates air pollution and can lead to breathing problems.

Running low

Our supply of fossil fuels is running low and may run out entirely in the next hundred years. In some areas, political disputes are also affecting people's access to fossil fuels. At the moment, most of our electricity supply and vehicles depend on fossil fuels. By switching over to alternative energy sources, such as solar power, the impact of running out of fossil fuels will be reduced. Even if the supply doesn't end, using cleaner sources of energy will be much better for the environment.

Natural gas

Natural gas is used as a fuel in power plants to generate electricity. It is also used for cooking and heating in many homes. Natural gas is one of the cleanest fossil fuels.

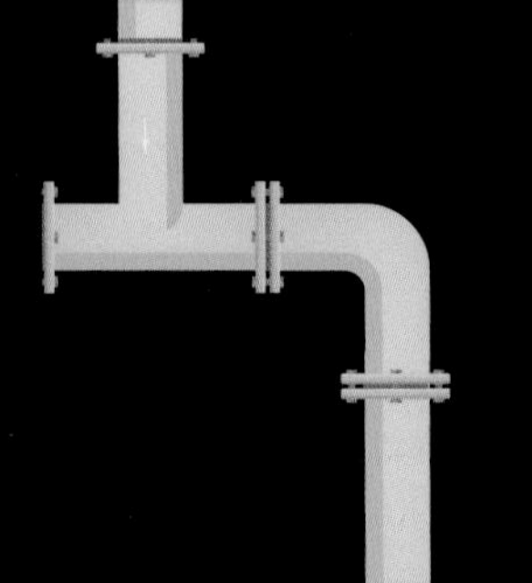

Location

Layers of gas are often found above or below oil **reserves** deep underground. Some gas is also dissolved in oil, but this can be extracted by processing the oil. The largest gas fields in the world are found in Russia, the Middle East, and the United States.

In the past

Up until the 1960s, natural gas wasn't used as often as other fossil fuels. It was difficult and expensive to transport. Most gas was burned as waste as soon as it came to the surface.

Gas is still burned as waste in places where it can't be collected, such as some offshore oil rigs.

Extracting gas

Today, gas is more widely used. It is extracted from the ground using pumps. Then it is sent to be processed through pipelines or transported in large tanks on vehicles. Once it has been processed, the gas is burned in power plants or it is packaged in smaller containers for home use.

Clean gas

Burning natural gas only creates water vapor and carbon dioxide. It does not release particulate matter or other types of air pollution, unlike other fossil fuels. For this reason, it is suitable for cooking and heating inside the home. However, it is very flammable, so it must be used with caution.

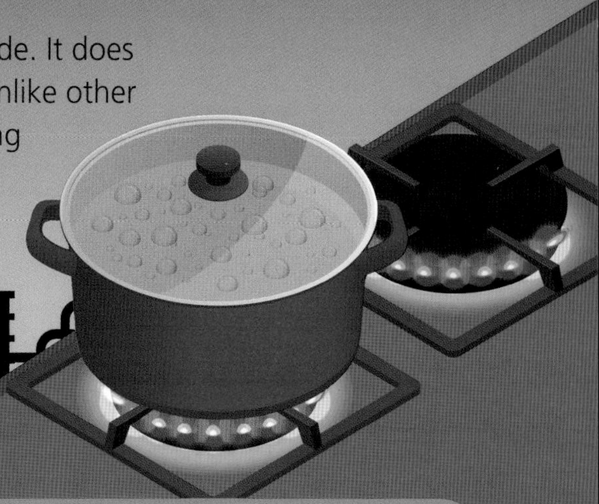

Burning natural gas produces ½ the carbon dioxide produced by burning oil.

Fracking

One way of extracting more gas is through fracking—drilling into **shale rock** to extract natural gas and oil. Water, sand, and chemicals are injected into rock at high pressure. This splits the rock apart, releasing the gas, which flows out through a well. Many people worry about the downsides of fracking, such as the increased risk of earthquakes, pollution, and the high use of water.

More and more

The supply of natural gas is fairly good, as it was not widely used in the past. However, our use of gas will probably increase in the future as supplies of other fossil fuels run low. Experts are looking for new techniques to extract gas from hard-to-reach places to ensure our supplies for the future.

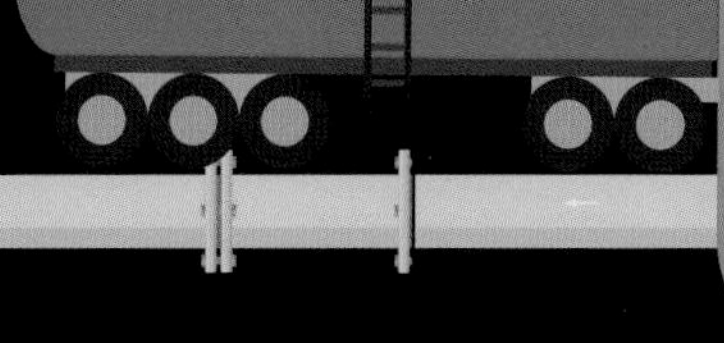

Nuclear power

Nuclear fuels, such as uranium and plutonium, are used to generate about 15 percent of the world's electricity. Nuclear energy does not contribute to the greenhouse effect, but it does have other serious risks.

Producing electricity

Nuclear fuels are not burned to generate electricity. Instead, the fuels are used in nuclear reactions that give off heat. This heat is used to drive a steam turbine that powers a generator, just as with fossil fuels (see page 7).

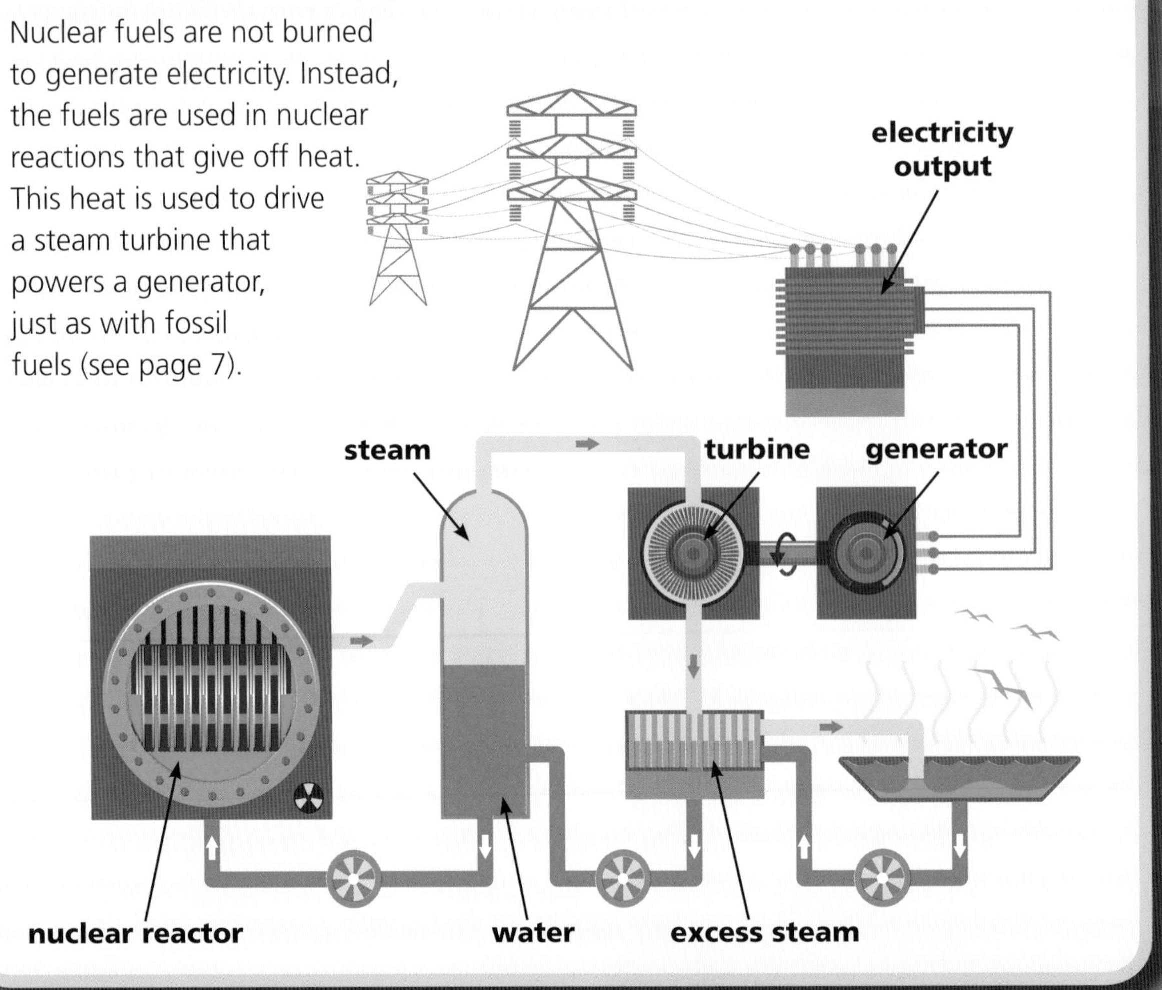

Benefits

Nuclear energy is considered a clean source of energy, as it does not give off carbon dioxide or contribute to air pollution. Nuclear power plants do not take up much space, unlike wind or solar farms, and they are relatively cheap to run. Nuclear fuels are nonrenewable, but there are still good reserves in areas such as Kazakhstan and Canada. These should last for hundreds of years if we continue using them at current rates.

Concerns

Nuclear fuels are **radioactive**, which means that they give off a dangerous form of energy called radiation. Living things can become very sick or even die if they are exposed to radiation. Nuclear fuels are still radioactive after they have been used, so nuclear waste has to be disposed of properly. It has to be buried deep underground in concrete to protect both people and the environment.

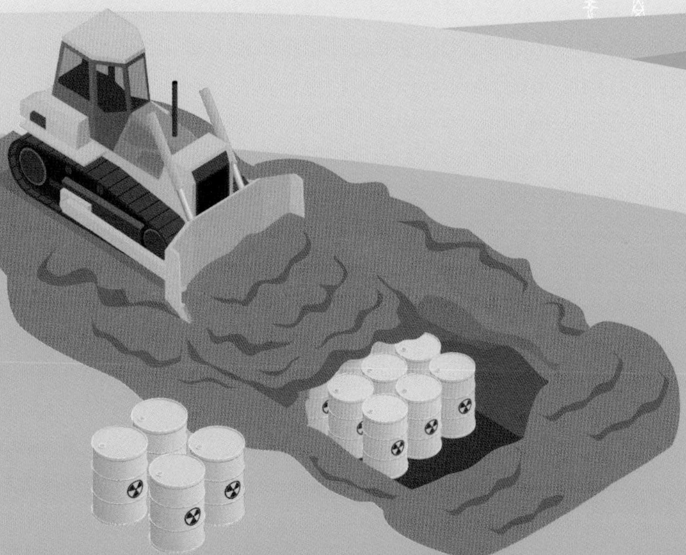

Accidents

Accidents at nuclear power plants can result in terrible disasters, in which large amounts of radioactive materials are released into the environment. Two of the most serious nuclear accidents happened at power plants in Fukushima, Japan, in 2011, and Chernobyl, Ukraine, in 1986. During these accidents, nuclear materials polluted nearby air, land, and water. It will not be safe for humans to return to these areas for many years.

Cases of cancer among children increased by 90 percent in Ukraine in the five years after the Chernobyl disaster.

A concrete cover has been built over the Chernobyl power plant to prevent further radiation from escaping.

Solar power

Solar power is a way of turning heat energy from sunlight into electricity. There are two methods—using solar panels and concentrating sunlight.

Solar panels

Standard solar panels contain 60 solar cells. Solar cells are made of photovoltaic materials, usually silicon, that create an electric current when exposed to light.

Panel placement

Solar panels can be found in many different places. Some homes and businesses have small rooftop panels that supply electricity for their own use. Huge numbers of panels are grouped together in solar farms, which provide enough electricity for towns. Panels can be attached to one place or programmed to follow the Sun across the sky so that they receive the maximum amount of light.

These solar panels provide electricity for an apartment block in Sydney, Australia.

Concentrating sunlight

In concentrated solar power plants, mirrors or magnifying glasses are used to reflect and concentrate sunlight in one place. This heat powers a steam turbine, like the ones used in fossil fuel power plants (see page 7).

Location

The best location for solar farms or concentrated solar power plants is dry tropical areas near the equator. These zones have many hours of sunshine per day all year that can generate a reliable supply of electricity.

Issues

One downside of solar power is that electricity can only be generated during the day, while it's sunny. This means that the electricity supply can be unreliable. Excess electricity needs to be stored to be used at night and during cloudy periods. Buying solar panels is also expensive, and many people and businesses can't afford the initial cost.

Increasing solar power

To encourage more people to use solar power, governments can subsidize the cost of solar panels to make them more affordable. The price of solar panels is dropping, as new, cheaper technology is created. However, in places such as the U.K., fossil fuel companies have lobbied governments to stop subsidizing panels, as they will lose money if people stop using fossil fuels.

One small step

Research schools that use solar panels for power. Investigate the costs of intalling them and whether your school could benefit from them.

California

California is an ideal location for solar power because of its sunny weather. It already has many individual solar panels, solar farms, and solar power plants, with plans for even more in the future.

Weather

The southern and inland parts of California have a warm, dry climate with many hours of sunlight. Desert areas are found across southeastern California. These are well suited to solar farms, as they experience almost no cloudy or rainy weather.

Home panels

Currently, around 20 percent of houses in California have solar panels. Soon, this number will rise dramatically, as all newly built homes in California will be required by law to have solar panels starting in 2020. This will be good for the environment, as people will be less dependent on fossil fuels. It will also save people money on their energy bills. However, some people are worried the additional price of panels will make homes too expensive.

Large-scale power

California is home to some of the world's largest solar farms. The Solar Star farm contains 1.7 million solar panels, spread across 5 square miles (13 sq km). It generates enough electricity to power over 250,000 homes. California also has huge concentrated solar power plants (see page 12), such as the Ivanpah plant—the largest of its kind in the world.

The Ivanpah concentrated solar power plant contains over 170,000 mirrors that reflect sunlight to three central towers.

16%
of California's electricity already comes from solar power.

Drawbacks

Solar farms take up a huge area of land. Their construction destroys desert habitats and affects the population of plants and animals that once lived there. The reflected beams of light in concentrated solar power plants also threaten wildlife. When birds fly through the scorching beams, they can be injured or even killed.

The future

By 2050, California plans to have 50 percent of its electricity supplied by renewable sources. Building more solar panels, both small- and large-scale, will help them achieve this goal. However, they must be careful not to destroy natural habitats at the same time.

Hydroelectric power

Hydroelectric power, or hydropower, is renewable energy generated by moving water. It is usually produced at dams.

Dams

Dams are barriers that restrict the flow of water from a river. If a dam is closed, a reservoir of water builds up behind the dam. If a dam is opened, the amount of water flowing through the dam can be controlled and used to generate electricity.

Generating electricity

Hydroelectric power plants are built on dams. When the dam is opened, water flows through it. This movement of water spins a turbine, which powers a generator. The generator makes electricity. Electricity is sent away from the dam through cables.

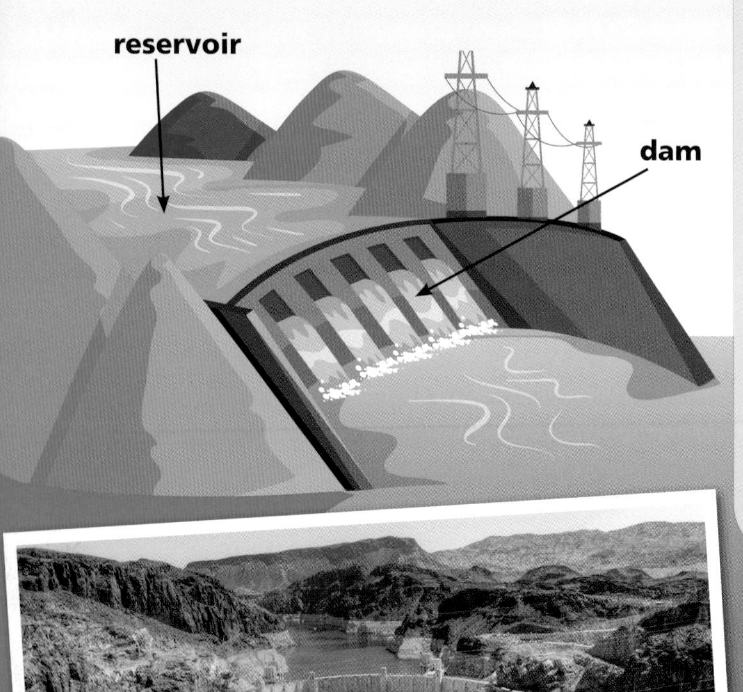

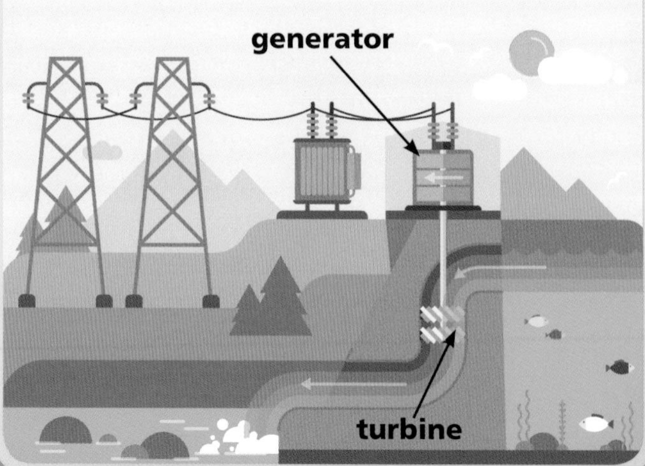

Around the world

Hydroelectric power plants are widely used around the world, in countries such as China, Canada, the U.S., and Russia. Large dams in these countries are capable of generating huge quantities of electricity. Hydroelectric dams are also popular in countries with many rivers. In Norway, 99 percent of all electricity is generated using hydropower.

Hoover Dam is a huge hydroelectric dam in Nevada and Arizona. Water gathers behind the dam to create the Lake Mead reservoir.

In 2016, over
16 percent
of all electricity generated globally came from hydropower.

Advantages

Hydroelectric power has many benefits. Water is a renewable resource and the process of using it to generate electricity creates no greenhouse gases, other than those produced during construction. Dams do not need to be replaced frequently—there are 100-year-old dams still working well! Water from the reservoir behind the dam can also be used for irrigation and household use.

Environmental impact

Building dams does alter the envonment. The construction of dams often leads to floods upstream, destroying **ecosystems** and people's homes. Communities have to relocate as their towns end up underwater once the river is dammed. If a dam breaks, it is a huge environmental disaster. The sudden floodwaters cover the surrounding area and can lead to deaths and millions of dollars in damage. When the Banqiao Reservoir Dam flooded in China in 1975, more than 170,000 people died.

Tidal power

The movement of water caused by Earth's tides also has potential for generating electricity. To capture tidal energy, a dam-like structure is built on the coast. It traps water at high tide and allows it to flow back out at low tide. However, tidal power isn't widely used at the moment, as the technology is still expensive and it is difficult to find suitable sites.

The Rance Tidal Power Station is built on an ***estuary*** *in northern France.*

FOCUS ON

The Itaipu Dam

The Itaipu Dam is one of the world's largest hydroelectric dams. It is located on the Paraná River, on the border between Brazil and Paraguay.

FACT FILE

LOCATION:
South America

HEIGHT:
643 feet (196 m)

LENGTH:
25,981 feet (7,919 m)

History

Brazil and Paraguay began discussing the idea of a hydroelectric dam in the 1960s. Both countries were interested in using the mighty Paraná River to generate power. The construction of the Itaipu Dam began in 1975. It was operational and generating power by 1984.

During periods of heavy rain, water is allowed to flow through the spillways on the left to avoid overloading the power plant.

spillways

BRAZIL
PARANÁ RIVER
PARAGUAY

Capacity

The Itaipu Dam can generate a huge amount of electricity, thanks to its 20 generators. In 2016, it set a world record for the most electricity produced in a year, generating 100 million megawatt hours (MWh). That's enough to meet Brazil's energy needs for 12 months and 18 days! Most of the electricity generated by the dam is used in Brazil, but a small amount is also supplied to Paraguay.

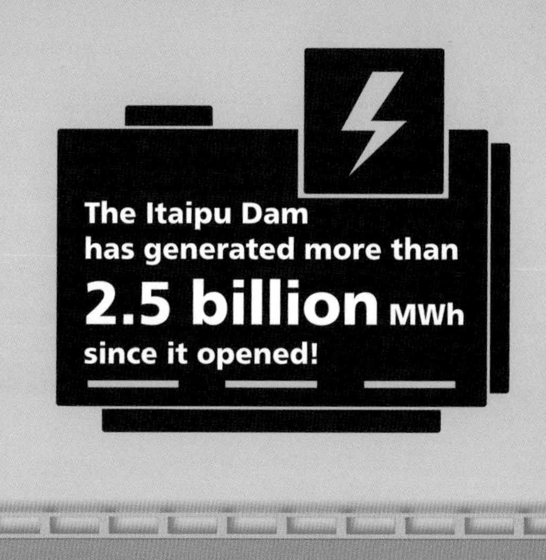

The Itaipu Dam has generated more than 2.5 billion MWh since it opened!

People

The construction of the Itaipu Dam has had a mixed impact on the people living nearby. Ten thousand families who lived along the Paraná River were forced to leave their homes in the early 1980s to avoid the risk of flooding. However, the project provided jobs for thousands of people during construction and employs over 3,000 people today.

Environmental impact

The Guaíra Falls waterfall was flooded during the construction of the dam. It had previously been one of the most powerful waterfalls by volume in the world. The waterfall had served as a barrier in the Paraná River, trapping certain species of animals and plants in different parts of the river. Now that it is gone, there are problems with invasive fish species moving along the river and competing with other species.

Biomass

Biomass is the name for plants and other organic matter that can be used as a source of energy. They are burned or processed into fuel, known as biofuels.

Sources

Wood is the most common type of biomass. It is burned as fuel in many places around the world. In agricultural areas, straw and unwanted plant matter are often burned as biomass. In the U.S. and Brazil, corn and sugarcane are grown on a huge scale to produce biofuels.

This tractor is carrying the outer leaves of sugarcane plants to be burned as biomass.

Burning biomass

Some types of biomass, including wood, straw and charcoal, are burned directly. In poorer areas of the world, people burn biomass for cooking and heating. Biomass is also burned in power plants to generate electricity. Coal power plants can be easily converted to burn biomass, which helps to reduce the use of coal.

Vehicle fuels

Some types of biomass can be processed into biofuels for vehicles and engines. Oil from the seeds of oil palm trees, rapeseed, and sunflowers, as well as waste cooking oil, can be turned into biodiesel. Bioethanol is made from sugarcane.

Biogas

Biogas is a naturally produced mixture of gases created by **decomposition**. It is made when bacteria break down organic waste, such as sewage or certain types of garbage in landfill sites. This gas can be collected in pipes and used as a fuel.

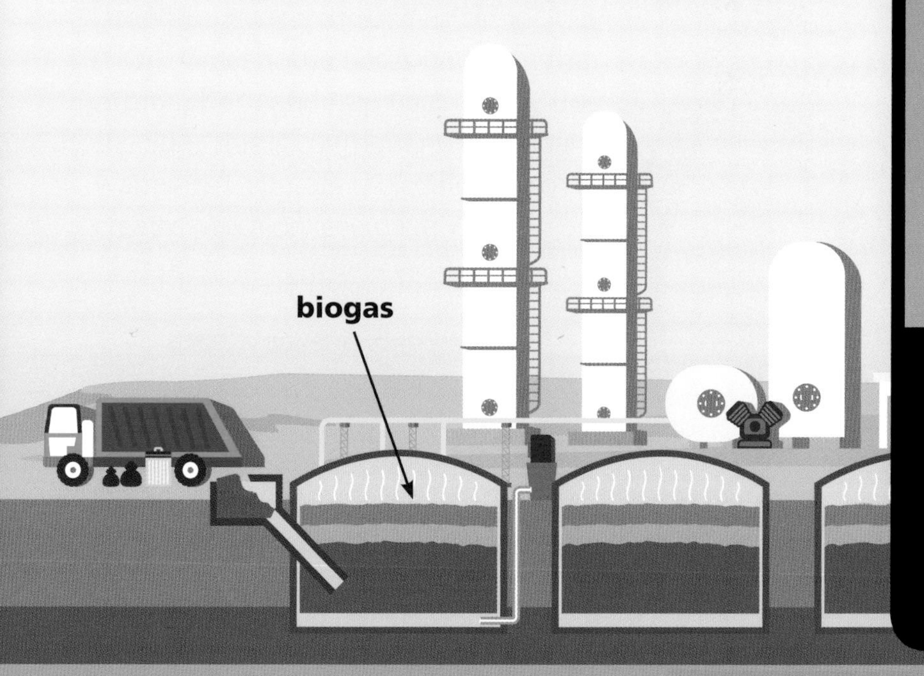

One small step

Some restaurants have an oil recycling service in which leftover cooking oil is turned into biodiesel. Encourage your favorite restaurant to join an oil recycling program.

Carbon dioxide

Burning biomass and biogas still creates air pollution and produces carbon dioxide, which adds to the greenhouse effect. However, the growing of new plants for biomass removes carbon dioxide from the atmosphere through **photosynthesis**.

Renewable source

Biomass is renewable, as we can always grow more crops. However, there are some drawbacks. Growing plants strictly for biomass may compete with food production—especially if a farmer can make more money from growing crops for fuel.

oxygen

carbon dioxide

Wind power

Wind power is a renewable and clean source of energy. However, the construction of wind turbines can have a negative impact on the surrounding area.

History

Wind has powered machines for thousands of years. In the past, windmills were used to pump water out of the ground and grind grain into flour. The movement of a windmill's blades (or sails) in the wind powered a machine inside the windmill.

Wind turbines

The design of a wind turbine is similar to that of a windmill. It has huge sails at the top of a tall tower. There is also a generator at the top of the tower. As the wind blows, the blades turn, which powers the generator and generates electricity.

One of the largest models of wind turbine can generate enough electricity in a year to power 600 U.S. homes for the same amount of time.

Wind farms

A group of turbines in one place is called a wind farm. Wind farms are built in windy areas, such as coastal or mountainous regions. Some homes and businesses have their own individual wind turbines.

This wind farm is built in the North Sea, off the northeast coast of England.

4 percent of the world's electricity is generated by wind power.

Positives

Wind is a renewable source of energy—it will never run out. Wind power is also considered a green source of energy, as it creates no air pollution. Generating electricity with wind power does not produce any greenhouse gases, other than those created by producing, transporting, and installing the turbines.

Negatives

The construction of wind turbines and farms is often **controversial**. They can be noisy and disturb people living nearby. Some people also consider them unattractive, and believe that they ruin views of the countryside. Birds can be killed by flying into the blades of a wind turbine. Wind power can also be an unreliable source of energy—however, the energy produced when there is wind can be stored for use during periods with less wind.

Geothermal energy

Geothermal energy is natural heat energy from deep inside Earth. It is used for heating and to generate electricity.

Less than 1 percent of global electricity production comes from geothermal energy.

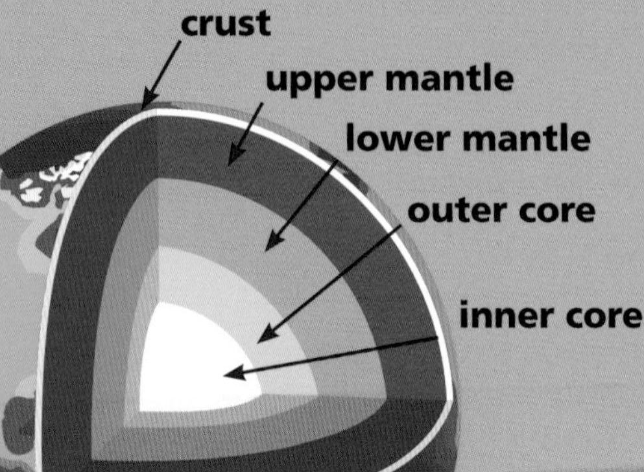

Structure

Earth is made up of several layers. The center, or core, is very hot. Heat from Earth's core travels out to the surface. It heats underground rocks and reservoirs of water.

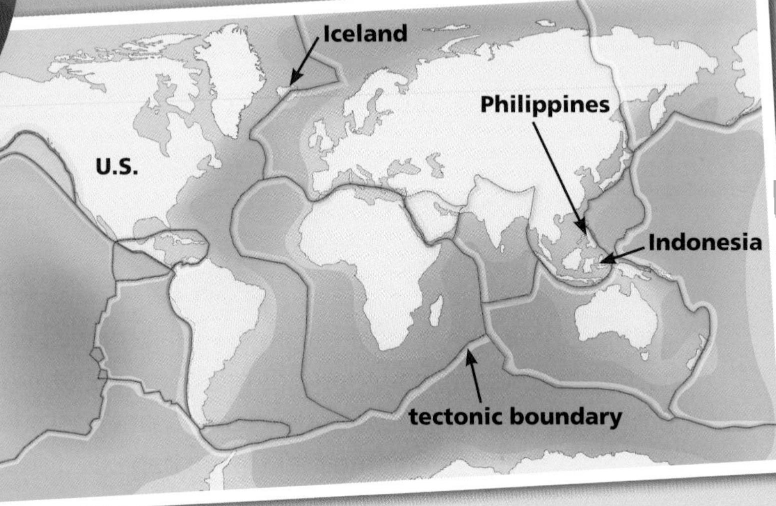

Location

Geothermal energy is easiest to access on the boundaries between the plates that make up the outer layer of Earth's crust. Here, Earth's heat is closer to the surface.

Over 20 countries located in these areas use geothermal energy, including Iceland (see pages 26–27), the U.S., the Philippines, and Indonesia.

Power plants

Geothermal power plants are similar to other power plants that use steam turbines (see page 7). However, the steam comes from different sources. One type of geothermal power plant uses hot water from deep underground. Steam from this water, which is around 356 °Fahrenheit (180 °C), powers the steam turbines. Once the water has cooled, it is then pumped back to be heated again.

hot water
hot water
cold water

Heating liquids

Another type of geothermal power plant uses hot water from underground to heat a liquid with a low boiling point, such as butane. The steam from the boiling butane is used to power the steam turbines. These power plants can be used in areas with less geothermal heat.

Heating

In areas with a lot of geothermal activity, such as Iceland (see pages 26–27), hot water from below ground can be piped directly into radiators and heating systems in homes and buildings. This saves the energy needed to heat the water. Air can also be pumped through warm or cold areas underground and then used to heat or cool buildings.

Benefits

Earth's heat will never be used up, so geothermal energy is renewable and sustainable, as long as the water used is returned underground. The process creates no air or water pollution.

Drawbacks

Geothermal energy does have disadvantages. Geothermal power plants are expensive to set up and can only be built in areas with geothermal activity. Although the process does not create pollution, a very small amount of greenhouse gases are brought to the surface when water is pumped from below ground.

FOCUS ON

Iceland

Iceland's unique location allows the country to take advantage of both geothermal and hydroelectric power. Geothermal energy is used to heat homes, while hydroelectric power is used to generate electricity.

Location

Iceland is an island in the north Atlantic Ocean. It is located on a tectonic plate boundary and over a volcanic hotspot, where there is more magma than usual. This results in a huge amount of geothermal activity.

History

In the past, Iceland generated electricity in fossil fuel power plants. This created a serious pollution problem on the island. It was also expensive, as the fossil fuels had to be imported from other countries. However, this pollution has disappeared since the island switched over to renewable sources of energy.

Heating homes

Geothermal energy is used to supply homes with heat and hot water. It is very easy to heat water and homes in this way, so energy bills are low. This is good for people trying to keep warm during the cold Icelandic winters.

Iceland also generates electricity using geothermal energy. This geothermal power plant is located in front of a geothermal hot lake.

Hot pools

Hot water from below ground comes to the surface in springs, geysers, and hot springs. Some have been turned into natural swimming pools where people can enjoy the warm water outdoors.

Hydropower

Iceland has many rivers and lakes. This allows the country to generate over 70 percent of its electricity supply in hydroelectric power plants. Much of this electricity is used by aluminum-processing plants, a main industry and source of income for Iceland. Many aluminum companies were attracted to Iceland by the low electricity costs available, thanks to hydroelectricity. This helped to boost the country's economy.

9 out of 10 homes in Iceland are heated with geothermal energy.

The future of energy

In the next 50 years, our energy resources will need to change. We do not have enough fossil fuels to continue depending on them as our main source of energy. We also need to switch over to clean sources of energy for environmental reasons.

Running low

If we continue to use them at current rates, we could run out of coal, oil, and natural gas within the next 100 years. At the moment, we are dependent on these fossil fuels to power the vehicles that we drive and the electricity that we use in industry and in our homes. If we start finding alternatives now to supplement our use, we will not reach a stage in which we run out of fossil fuels entirely.

Environmental damage

The environmental impact of using fossil fuels is getting worse every day. Ecosystems are being destroyed to extract fossil fuels, pollution is damaging the health of living things, and the greenhouse gases released are causing our climate to change.

Clean power in poorer countries

Replacing fossil fuel power plants with renewable, clean power plants can be very expensive. Many poorer countries cannot afford to do this. They depend on their current fossil fuel power plants for electricity to power homes and businesses that make money for the country. Many are exploring lower-cost energy options such as micro-hydro projects and solar projects.

Tropical areas are ideal locations for solar power, due to their many hours of sunlight. Thanks to foreign aid, small communities, such as this one in Zimbabwe, can set up solar panels to generate electricity for homes and businesses.

Making a change

Industries and governments are responsible for making the changes that will have the biggest impact on the energy that we use, such as investing in cleaner power plants. Find out what your government is doing to support clean energy. If they aren't doing enough, write an email asking them to consider investing in the future.

One small step

Research your home energy supplier and find out if they use renewable energy sources. Is it possible for the company to switch to more environmentally friendly sources of energy?

At home

We can all make small changes that will make a difference. Be careful with the electricity you consume. Turn off lights or electrical devices when you leave a room. Wear a sweater instead of turning up the heat.

Glossary

atmosphere The layer of gases around Earth

biomass Plants, wood, or waste used as fuel

controversial A topic that is argued over

decomposition When something breaks down

ecosystem All the living things in an area

estuary An area where a river flows into an ocean or sea

extract To take something out

fossil fuel A fuel that comes from the ground, such as coal, oil, or gas

geothermal The heat inside Earth

greenhouse effect The effect when certain gases gather in Earth's atmosphere, trapping the Sun's heat close to the surface and making it warmer

greenhouse gas A gas that traps heat in the atmosphere, such as carbon dioxide

nonrenewable Describes something that can't be reproduced and can run out

photosynthesis The process by which plants generate energy using sunlight and carbon dioxide

radioactive Describes something that gives off harmful radiation

renewable Describes something that can be reproduced and will not run out

reserve The amount of something that is left

shale rock A type of rock that easily breaks into layers

sustainable Describes something that can continue for a long time because it does not harm the environment

turbine A machine that produces power by using something to turn a wheel

Learning More

Books

Dyer, Janice. ***Designing Green Communities.*** Crabtree Publishing, 2018.

Mangor, Jodie. ***Geothermal Energy.*** Core Library, 2016.

Stuckey, Rachel. ***Energy from Living Things: Biomass Energy.*** Crabtree Publishing, 2016.

Websites

climatekids.nasa.gov/power-up/
Play a game to power a city with renewable energy.

video.nationalgeographic.com/video/101-video-shorts/fossil-fuels-climate-change
Watch a video about fossil fuels.

www.ovoenergy.com/blog/green/20-fascinating-renewable-energy-facts.html
Find out 20 facts about renewable energy.

Index